The Story of the First Christmas

Pictures by Pamela Johnson

Adapted from the Gospel According to Matthew and from the Gospel According to Luke

HarperCollins*Publishers*

This story takes place about 2,000 years ago in the part of the world that is now called Israel. Two cities are important to the story: Nazareth, in Galilee, to the north; and Bethlehem, in Judea, to the south.

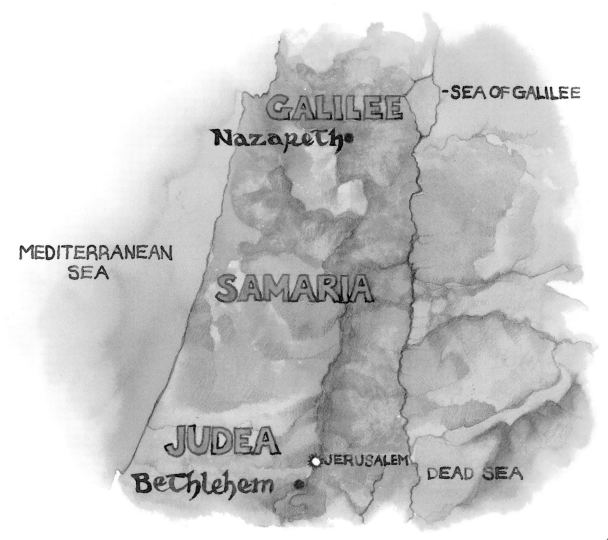

In Nazareth there lived a young woman named Mary. Mary was engaged to marry a man named Joseph, who had come from Bethlehem.

One day God sent the angel Gabriel to Nazareth to visit Mary. Mary was frightened.

But Gabriel said, "Do not be afraid, Mary, for you have found favor with God. You will give birth to a son, and you shall call him Jesus."

Mary said to the angel, "How can this be?"

Gabriel said to her, "The Holy Spirit will come upon you, and the power of the Most High will overshadow you. The child to be born will be called holy, the Son of God."

And Mary said, "Let it be according to your word."

An angel of the Lord appeared also to Joseph, in a
dream. The angel said, "There is a baby growing inside
Mary. It is the child of the Holy Spirit. Mary will give
birth to a son, and you shall call him Jesus."

Now, at that time, Galilee and Judea were part of the vast Roman Empire. Caesar Augustus, the Roman Emperor, announced a census. Every man had to go, with his family, to the city of his birth in order to be counted for taxes. So Joseph and Mary traveled from Nazareth to Bethlehem.

In Bethlehem there was no room for Joseph and Mary at the inn, so they had to sleep in the stable with the animals. In the middle of the night, Jesus was born, and Mary wrapped him in swaddling clothes and laid him in a manger.

Nearby there were shepherds in the field, keeping watch over their flock. An angel of the Lord appeared to them, and the glory of the Lord shone around them, and they were filled with fear.

But the angel said, ''Be not afraid. I bring you good news of a great joy for all the people. This day is born in Bethlehem a Savior, who is Christ the Lord. And this will be a sign for you: You will find a babe wrapped in swaddling clothes and lying in a manger.''

11

Suddenly there was with the angel a multitude of the
heavenly host praising God and saying, "Glory to God
in the highest, and on earth peace, good will toward men."

After the angels returned to heaven, the shepherds said to one another, "Let us go to Bethlehem and see this child."

The shepherds went with great haste and found Mary and Joseph, and the baby lying in the manger.

After the shepherds saw Jesus, they told everyone they met what they had seen and heard. And everyone was filled with wonder at what the shepherds reported.

Then the shepherds returned to their fields, glorifying and praising God.

Soon after Jesus was born, three wise men came from the East. They had seen a bright star in the sky and knew it meant that the child of God had come. They followed the star until it shone directly above the stable where Jesus lay.

Then they went in and saw the child with Mary, his mother, and they fell down and worshiped him.

Joy to the world!